Hey Diddle Diddle

UNIT 16

By Marilyn Sprick and Jessica Sprick

Illustrated by Steve Clark

Main Characters

This is the dog.
Who is this? (The dog)

This is the cat.
Who is this? (The cat)

This is the cow.
Who is this? (The cow)

Table of Contents
Hey Diddle Diddle

STORY 1, DUET STORY

Introduction 1

Hey Diddle Diddle is an old favorite Nursery Rhyme.

STORY 1, DUET STORY

Chapter 1, What We Want 2

Three poor animals wish for their dreams to come true.

STORY 2, SOLO STORY

Chapter 2, I Wish 5

The cat, the dog, and the cow wish, wish, wish!

STORY 3, DUET STORY

Chapter 3, Mother Goose Sends Help 8

The cat, the dog, and the cow meet Mother Goose.

STORY 4, SOLO STORY

Chapter 4, The Cat and the [fiddle] 11

It is time for the cat to make his wish!

STORY 5, DUET STORY

Chapter 5, The [dog] **and the** [cow] 13

The dish grants two more wishes.

STORY 6, SOLO STORY

Chapter 6, Wish, Wish, Wish 16

Hear one fiddle-playing cat and one laughing dog. See one jumping cow.

DUET STORIES: Adults read the small text. Students read the large text.

Hey Diddle Diddle

INTRODUCTION

Nursery Rhymes have been around for a very long time. An old, old favorite is *Hey Diddle Diddle*. It goes like this.

Hey diddle . . . diddle,
The cat and the . . . fiddle,
The cow jumped over the . . . moon;

The little dog laughed to see such . . . sport,

while the dish ran away with the . . . spoon.

I'll say the rhyme again. See if you can fill in the words when I pause.

Look at the picture. Steve Clark illustrated this storybook.
Touch the cat. What is the cat doing? (Playing a fiddle)
Touch the cow. What is the cow doing? (Jumping over the moon)
Touch the dog. What is the dog doing? (Laughing)
Touch the dish and the spoon. What is the dish doing? (Running away with the spoon)

Hey Diddle Diddle

CHAPTER 1 • WHAT WE WANT

Once upon a time in Mother Goose Land, there lived a cat, a dog, and a cow. The animals were poor and often did not have enough to eat. But like all animals, they had dreams.

The cat said,

"I wish I had a  .

I would play country music. Yee ha!"

What did the cat want? (He wanted a fiddle. He wanted to play country music.)

The  said, "I wish I could

jump over the moon. I could see the universe and tell wonderful stories!"

What did the cow want? (The cow wanted to see the universe. She wanted to tell wonderful stories.)

The  said, "I wish I could laugh.

Laughter is a golden sound."

Poor little dog. Try as he might, all he could do was howl.

"Woo, woo, wooooooo."

What did the dog want? (The dog wanted to laugh.)

STORY 1, DUET

Yes, it was a hard life, but the animals had their dreams.

The cat said, "I want to play music so everyone can dance."

The  said, "I want to jump over the moon."

The said, "Woo, woo, wooooo. I want to laugh."

When things were tough, the cat pretended to play the fiddle. The cow practiced jumping, and the dog tried laughing. At least they had their dreams.

What kept the animals from being sad when times were hard? (They had their dreams.)

CHAPTER 2
I Wish

The cat sat in the tree.

"," said the cat. "See the moon!"

"I see the moon too," said the . "I wish. I wish I could . . ."

What did the cow want? (The cow wanted to jump over the moon.)

The 🐶 was sad. He said,
"Woo, woo, wooooo.
I wish I could . . ."

What did the dog want? (He wanted to be able to laugh.)

The cat said, "I wish. I wish I had a  ."

What did the cat want? (The cat wanted a fiddle.)

CHAPTER 3
Mother Goose Sends Help

Mother Goose was flying south to spend her winter days in a warmer place. She stopped by the little village where the cat, the dog, and the cow lived. Mother Goose could see that the animals were sad.

What was the problem? (The animals were sad.)

Mother Goose said,

"<u>Dear me</u>. <u>I see a sad</u> , <u>a sad cat</u>, <u>and a sad</u> ."

Mother Goose said to the cat, the dog, and the cow,

"<u>Meet me soon</u>

when the moon is full."

What do you think Mother Goose is going to do?

The three animals gathered near the village square.

"I see the moon," said the cat.

"I wonder what Mother Goose wants."

Soon the goose appeared.

 said, "This is too sad.

I have sent for the dish and the spoon. When they arrive, you will each be granted one wish. Remember, winter is near. Think carefully. You each have only one wish."

What do you think the animals will wish for?

That was all the goose had to say. Then she flew quickly away to spend her winter days in a warmer place. The animals were quite excited.

Cat looked down the road. "Look," he said.

"I see the dish and the ."

What do you think the dish and the spoon will do? (The dish and the spoon will give each of the animals a wish.)

CHAPTER 4

The Cat and the

Who is this chapter about? (The cat)

"Moo, moo, moo," said the .

"Woo, woo, wooooo," said the .

"See the dish and the ," said the cat.

What did the cat see? (The dish and the spoon)
How do you think the cat felt? (Happy, excited . . .)

The cat said, "I wish I had a ."

The dish said, "A  it is!"

The cat was .

What happened in this chapter? (The cat got a fiddle. The cat got his wish.)

CHAPTER 5

The  and the

"Wow," said the cow.

"The cat has a ."

What did the cat get? (The cat got a fiddle. The cat got his wish.)

"That's right," said the dish, "and what do you wish?"

The  said, "I wish I could

jump over the moon."

The dish said,

"Jump cow, jump." And so he did! The cow jumped right over the moon.

"Woo, woo, wooooo," howled the dog.

"That was cool! You made that cow jump over the moon?"

What did the cow get? (The cow got to jump over the moon. The cow got her wish.)

"That's right," said the dish, "and what do you wish?"

The  said, "I wish I could laugh. Laughter makes the world go round."

Then the spoon said, "Laugh, little dog." The little dog opened his mouth and out came . . .

"Tee hee, tee hee, tee hee."

What did the dog get?

(The dog got to laugh. He got his wish.)

"I am ," chorused both the cat and the dog.

"Me too," said the

from the other side of the moon.

"We are glad," said the dish and the spoon. Then the dish and the spoon waved good bye and ran off to grant more wishes.

The winter was cold and times were hard, but the animals had their dreams. The cat played his fiddle. The little dog laughed, and the cow had adventures on the other side of the moon.

How did the cat, the cow, and the dog feel? (Happy) Why?

CHAPTER 6

Wish, Wish, Wish

"I had I wish," said the cat. "Hear me."

"I had I wish," said the . "Moo moo. See me."

"I had I wish," said the . "Hear me. Tee hee, tee hee!"

"I am 🙂," said the dish. "Me too," said the 🥄.

Why were the dish and the spoon happy? (They made the cat, the dog, and the cow happy.)
What do you think the dish and the spoon will do in the next village?

UNIT 1
*I
I

UNIT 2
2
see

UNIT 3
me
I'm

UNIT 4
am
Sam

UNIT 5
sad
Dad
*said
3

UNIT 6
Dee
*the
mad

UNIT 7
and
man
seem

UNIT 8
Tamee
meet
that
sat
seems

UNIT 9
we
need
seeds
sweet
Nan
at
weeds
*was
weed

UNIT 10
Tim
sit
in
Matt
sees
Tam
did

UNIT 11
this
*is
Dan
he
*his
Ann
Nat
needs
it
had
an

UNIT 12
cat
can
*has
meets
scat
*wasn't
*a
cats
hit

UNIT 13
ran
trees
*want
can't
win
rat
deer
three
tee hee
near
tree
didn't

UNIT 14
*would
*could
sea
sand
eat
treats
hear
*as
treat
Dean
*with
swam
she
swim
wish
seen
*isn't
*should
neat

UNIT 15
think
hid
'smack
seat
*couldn't
trick
it's
eats
snack
wink
*he's

UNIT 16
woo
*to
moon
too
dear
noon
dish
moo